Contents

Pavilion Publishing and Media

Pavilion inspires individuals to change lives – both their own and others' – through professional, workforce and personal development publications across public sectors of civil society that support, safeguard and educate communities.

Pavilion is the leading publisher of professional development products and services for public, private and voluntary workers in the health, social care, education and community safety sectors.

We believe that everyone has the right to fulfil their potential and we strive to supply products and services that help raise standards, promote best practice and support continuing professional development.

The Pavilion Publishing brand

Pavilion was established in 1986 and initially produced training materials in the social and health care sectors. We gradually expanded to cover events and other publications, including magazines. We have recently increased our portfolio to include education and the community safety sectors and we continue to extend our range of services through innovative approaches to the market.

Introduction

Care Quality Guides

Pavilion's Care Quality Guides aim to help you refresh, develop or extend your learning in key areas of practice.

- If you are new to working with a particular client group or in a new role, you can use the material to quickly develop knowledge you will need, and where appropriate, work towards a relevant qualification.
- If you are a more experienced worker, you can use the guides to refresh your learning, and to contribute towards your continuing professional development.
- If you are a manager, you can use these guides with staff to meet your responsibilities for providing induction and staff supervision, and opportunities for training and development and continuing professional development. This will contribute towards meeting Care Quality Commission (CQC) Standards.

Maintaining and improving your knowledge and skills

This guide can help towards maintaining and improving your knowledge and skills.

You can work through the guide, section by section, completing the **thinking activities** as you go.

Supervision and continuing professional development (CPD)

This guide can be used for continuing professional development. If you are a manager, you might like to ask your staff members to work through it section by section, completing the **thinking activities** each contains. Their responses can be discussed as part of on-going supervision, and on completion of the guide, you can both fill in the CPD certificate at the end.

Meeting the Care Quality Commission (CQC) Standards

If you are a manager or provider of a health and social care service, you can use this guide for staff development in order to contribute towards meeting current training standards and to prepare for quality checks and inspections. In particular, using this guide with your staff will contribute towards ensuring that they have training and CPD opportunities to strengthen and develop their skills and knowledge.

Qualifications Credit Framework (QCF)

Using this guide can also contribute towards social care qualifications. It provides underpinning knowledge for unit LD 307 Principles of Supporting Individuals with a Learning Disability Regarding Sexuality and Sexual Health, and the thinking activities can contribute to evidence of learning. The following table maps the content to the QCF learning outcomes. NB. Pavilion also publishes a QCF workbook that covers all the learning outcomes and includes assessment questions and an evidence log. There is an accompanying training pack which can be used by managers and trainers for QCF training or for CPD (full information can be found at www.pavpub.com).

Terminology

The following terms are used throughout this guide.

People – (female or male) Including adults and children with learning disabilities

Staff – Anyone who has a paid role supporting people with learning disabilities (eg. care staff, support workers, managers and professionals)

Family carer – A relative who provides support

Carer – A staff member or a family carer

How the content of this guide maps to the QCF unit LD307 Principles of Supporting Individuals with a Learning Disability Regarding Sexuality and Sexual Health

Content of guide	LD307 Learning outcome (LO)
Section 1: The development of human sexuality	LO1: Understand the development of human sexuality
Section 2: The sexual development of individuals with a learning disability	LO2: Understand how the sexual development of individuals with a learning disability can differ
Section 3: Issues of sexual health and how these can be supported	LO3: Understand the issues of sexual health and how these can be supported
Section 4: Relevant legislation	LO4: Understand relevant legislation influencing the support of sexuality and sexual health for individuals with learning disabilities
Section 5: Supporting the sexual expression of an individual with a learning disability	LO5: Know how to support the sexual expression of an individual with a learning disability

Section 1

The development of human sexuality

Introduction

As you read through this booklet there may be things that make you uncomfortable or embarrassed. This is to be expected as we do not often talk explicitly about sex. It may also be because it brings up issues in your own sexual life. If things are worrying you, do talk to someone. This could be a family member, a colleague or a friend. You could also contact one of the advice lines in the Useful contacts section.

Defining the terms

Sexuality

The term 'sexuality' means different things to different people. It can mean the capacity for sexual feelings, or a person's sexual orientation or preference. For example, sometimes when people talk about their sexuality they are talking about whether they are lesbian, gay, bisexual or heterosexual. However, these terms are describing sexual identities.

Thinking activity

Using the WHO definition, write a list of things that could improve the sexual health of individuals and communities.

Sexual identity is part of a person's sexuality, but sexuality can cover other things too. It can refer to:

- a person's gender: whether they see themselves as female or male
- a person's sexual desires
- a person's sexual experiences
- the way a person behaves and dresses.

In other words, sexuality can cover all 'aspects of personal and social life which have erotic significance' (Jackson & Scott, 1996).

Sexual health

Sexual health is more than not having sexually transmitted diseases. It may involve:

- being able to make choices about sex
- being able to enjoy sex
- the ability to produce children
- the prevention and treatment of sexually transmitted diseases.

The World Health Organization (WHO) gives the following definition:

'*Sexual health is a state of physical, mental and social well-being in relation to sexuality. It requires a positive and respectful approach to sexuality and sexual relationships, as well as the possibility of having pleasurable and safe sexual experiences, free of coercion, discrimination and violence.*' (WHO, 2014)

The WHO definition talks about the possibility and not a right to sex. No one has a right to have sex with another person unless the other person agrees.

Many people with learning disabilities have poor sexual health because:

- they have been taught to feel guilty about sexual feelings
- they are discouraged from having sexual relationships
- a large number of them have been sexually abused

- they have been given little information about sexually transmitted diseases
- there may be problems with their sexual response system linked a syndrome they have or medication they are taking.

Your role of supporting people with learning disabilities should promote their sexual health.

Sexual orientation

Sexual orientation is about whether a person is interested emotionally, romantically or sexually in people of the same or opposite sex. The main terms are:

- heterosexual – interested in people of the opposite sex
- homosexual – interested in people of the same sex
- bisexual – interested in both women and men
- asexual – lack of interest in sex with either men or women.

Research has suggested that sexual orientation lies on a continuum, as seen in the diagram below.

Sexual expression

Like sexuality, 'sexual expression' is used to mean a wide range of things. If an individual is expressing themselves sexually, they are doing sexual things where other people are involved. It is not just limited to sexual acts with other people, but includes dressing or acting in a way that may be seen as sexual by others.

Sexual expression is about how a person chooses to present themselves or what sex they choose to have. The desire for sexual expression will be much more important for some people than others and it can change over time. However, too often certain groups of people are assumed to be uninterested in expressing themselves sexually. This includes people with learning disabilities, but also older people. This is partly due to highly sexualised media images, for example underwear adverts usually show attractive, able-bodied young people.

Sexual development milestones

Early childhood and gender identity

During infancy it is normal for children to explore their bodies, including touching their genitals and enjoying being naked. It is also common to find baby boys with erections.

Between the ages of two and three, most children will have an understanding of whether they are a girl or a boy, which will be initially linked to whether they have a penis or a vagina. By the time they go to school their gender identity will be firmly established, as well as their understanding of gender roles. The messages that children get about gender roles can be very varied. They may encounter more traditional ideas about what it is to be a man or a woman from some people, while other people may offer more progressive views.

As a child's knowledge of gender roles develops, so may their sense of not conforming to them – of being different. Some children may choose to hide this difference while others may be unwilling or unable to do so. Among children who feel different, some will be transgender – feeling that they are not the gender that their body suggests. Some children who feel different may later have a lesbian, gay or bisexual identity, while others will feel secure in a heterosexual identity.

The cognitive ability of children with learning disabilities may mean that it takes them longer to learn about gender identity and gender roles. Some may need explicit teaching to help them understand the differences between females and males. Also depending on cognitive ability, some children with learning disabilities may start to notice their difference to other children in early childhood. This may include what they are unable to do in comparison to their peers or how they are treated differently.

Thinking activity

What differences may there be in the roles expected of children with learning disabilities when they reach adulthood compared to other children?

Puberty

Puberty is triggered by hormones in the brain and sexual organs. It leads to changes in the brain, muscles, blood, skin, hair, breasts and sexual organs. Many of the changes during puberty are to prepare the body for sexual reproduction.

For girls, puberty is marked by the start of menstruation – the menarche. Typically this is when a girl is 12 or 13 years old. Other physical signs are the development of breasts, pubic hair and a change in body shape caused by the hips widening and a change in fat distribution.

For boys, puberty is marked by the first ejaculation. On average, this is when a boy is 13 years old. Before this age, is it common for boys to wake up with erections or to have them spontaneously at different times of the day. Other changes for boys during puberty are an increase in the size of the testes and scrotum leading the 'balls' to drop in their sack. Hair develops on different parts of the body including the pubic area, chest, underarms and face. The voice drops due to the growth of the larynx and the Adam's apple can become prominent. There are increases in bone size – particularly the jaw and the shoulders – and muscle mass.

Awareness of sexual orientation

Most children grow up with the people around them assuming that they are or will be heterosexual. For example, a mother may talk to her young daughter about getting married in the future and a father may give his son advice about dating girls. These conversations rarely start with 'If you are heterosexual...'. The majority of children will go on to have heterosexual relationships and so such conversations make sense and are unlikely to cause any anxiety, though they might be embarrassing.

Growing up with a different sexual identity, the young person will have to manage the assumptions and expectations made about their sexual identity, which conflict with how they might see themselves. This can cause a lot of stress. Society is now more accepting of gay and lesbian people, enabling many people to feel comfortable in their identity and to 'come out' about their sexual orientation. However, experiences of being ostracised or needing to repress their identity are still common.

The point at which people are aware of their sexual identity can vary enormously. Some lesbians and gay men know in early childhood, while others do not realise until well into adulthood.

First sexual experience with another person

A person's first sexual experience can be a very significant life event, however it is not always a good experience. People have different ideas about what counts as their first sexual experience. For example, some people only count sexual contact that involves penetrative vaginal sex. This is emphasised by the notion of virginity, particularly for women. In the UK, about a quarter of 15 year olds report having had sex, and about 80% will have done so by the end of their teenage years (Channel 4, 2008).

Many people are critical about their first sexual experience. This does not necessarily mean that they regret it, but rather that they identify how much more they had to learn about sex. This is important to remember when supporting people with learning disabilities who should similarly be allowed to learn through experience.

Ongoing sexual relationships

Having an ongoing sexual relationship with someone is highly valued in society and usually it is expected that neither person will be having other sexual relationships. This is a common expectation of both dating and marriage. However, for some people their relationship will not be exclusive and this may be an agreement between the couple.

Some people hope to have only one long-term sexual relationship in their life while other people are more pragmatic and expect to have a number of sexual relationships.

There are potential benefits to having a long-term sexual relationship. These include:

- the opportunity for regular sex with another person
- learning how best to enjoy sex through repeated opportunities with the same person
- the development of trust, companionship, intimacy and love
- the opportunity to have children.

There are also risks of having a long-term sexual relationship, including:

- distress if the relationship ends
- dishonesty
- feeling obliged to have sex
- putting up with being treated badly out of fear of losing the relationship
- feeling trapped by the expectations of being in a relationship.

Pregnancy and becoming a parent

Pregnancy and childbirth are significant milestones in a woman's sexual development. From a biological point of view, this could be seen as the goal or end point of sexual development. The physical implications of pregnancy and childbirth on a woman's body are significant.

Sex between women and men may or may not be linked to the hope of pregnancy. The availability of contraception has meant that heterosexual sex can be enjoyed with little risk of an unwanted pregnancy. However, not everyone supports the use of contraception. For example, many Catholics believe that sex should only be about having children and resist the use of contraception as it divorces sex from procreation.

Artificial insemination and in vitro fertilisation are increasingly common means of conceiving. This applies not only to heterosexual couples where there are fertility issues, but also to women who are single or in lesbian relationships.

Menopause

The menopause generally occurs when women are in their late 40s or early 50s. It is the outcome of changes in sexual hormones marking the end of a woman's fertility. The hormone changes can be linked to:

- irregular periods
- hot flushes and night sweats
- mood changes and stress
- vaginal dryness
- tenderness of the breasts
- osteoporosis (weakening of bones).

Some women do not experience any of these problems, but those who do can experience negative effects on their physical and mental health. There are a number of treatment options that can be considered if the symptoms are adversely affecting a woman's quality of life. Hormone replacement therapy (HRT) is the leading treatment.

The term 'male menopause' is sometimes used to describe changes in male sex hormones. The level of testosterone may gradually decrease as men age. Testosterone levels may also decline faster due to disease, for example, diabetes. Treatment may be offered if there are physical or mental difficulties associated with low levels of testosterone.

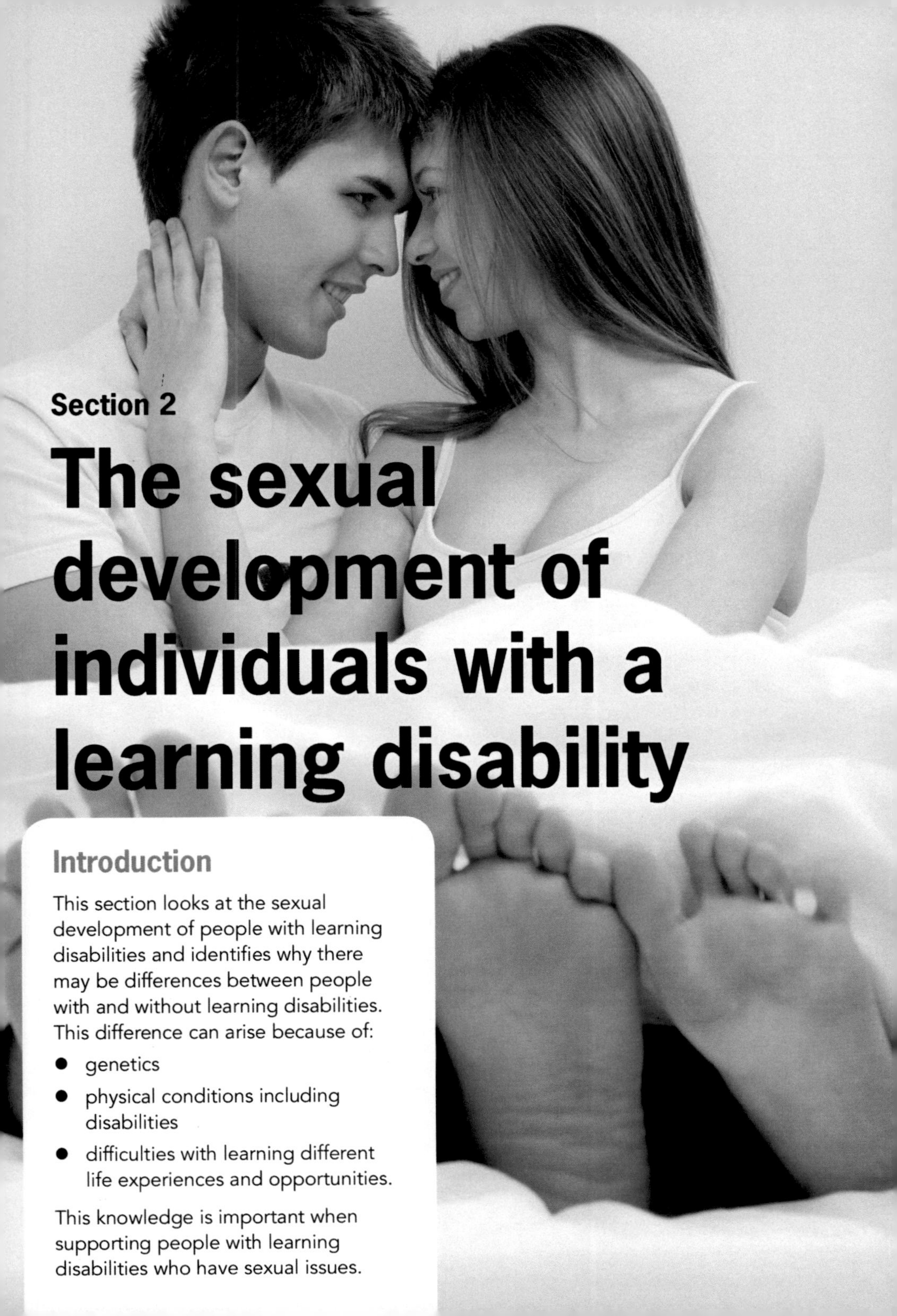

Section 2

The sexual development of individuals with a learning disability

Introduction

This section looks at the sexual development of people with learning disabilities and identifies why there may be differences between people with and without learning disabilities. This difference can arise because of:

- genetics
- physical conditions including disabilities
- difficulties with learning different life experiences and opportunities.

This knowledge is important when supporting people with learning disabilities who have sexual issues.

Genetic factors

Genetic conditions are one of the four known causes of learning disability. The other factors are problems during pregnancy or birth and health conditions during childhood. In about a third of cases the cause of a learning disability is not known.

Note: The following information is only relevant if you are supporting someone who has a known genetic condition – this is only a minority of people with learning disabilities.

Puberty and reproduction

Some genetic conditions affect puberty and can cause infertility. People with some syndromes are able to have children but the chance of this happening is very low. For example, people with Down's syndrome are known to have reduced fertility. However, limited opportunities for sex and the prevalence of women with Down's syndrome on contraception are factors that explain why parents with Down's syndrome are so rare.

There are still gaps in our knowledge about the most common syndromes. For example, it has been noticed that baby boys with Down's syndrome generally have smaller penises and are less likely to have spontaneous erections. It is likely that this might cause difficulties with masturbation for some boys as they go through puberty, but there is not yet enough research in this area.

Some of the more common syndromes affecting people with learning disabilities include:

- Down's syndrome
- Prader-Willi syndrome
- Fragile X syndrome
- Turner's syndrome
- William's syndrome

Masturbation

Most often, attention is given to masturbation and men but it is important not to overlook the needs of women in this area.

Puberty may be different for people with some syndromes, which may affect a person with a learning disabilities' ability to masturbate as there may be problems with arousal and orgasm. With males, there are physical signs: difficulty getting and maintaining an erection, and not ejaculating. It is much more difficult to know if

Thinking activity

Using the internet, find out how puberty may be affected for people with Angelman syndrome.

Can women with this syndrome have children?

females are experiencing problems with masturbation and arousal.

We should not assume that a person with a particular syndrome will be able to masturbate. For example, it should be assumed that people with Prader-Willi syndrome will have problems with masturbation. There are other common reasons why people with learning disabilities have problems with masturbation.

Thinking activity

What are your thoughts about people with learning disabilities masturbating?

Medication

A known side effect of many medicines is an effect on the sexual response system. More is known about how drugs may affect men than women. The risk of sexual dysfunction is common with anti-epileptic medicines, for example carbamazepine. Antipsychotic medicines are sometimes prescribed to people with learning disabilities who have challenging behaviour. They also have sexual side effects.

Drugs can have other side effects linked to sexuality. For example, sodium valproate (an anti-epileptic medication) can impact on a woman's periods. When supporting a person with learning disabilities who is taking medication it is good practice to be aware of the possible side effects.

Physical disability

A person's physical disability can make it very difficult to masturbate. Masturbation can require fine motor control, which some people do not have. If a person is unable to eat unaided, for example, it can be assumed that they will have physical difficulties masturbating.

Incontinence pads for some people will act as a barrier to masturbating. The person may not be able to remove a pad or move a hand inside it adequately. Sometimes carers will deliberately use clothing to stop a person from touching themselves, for example tight-fitting clothing or an overall. This may be a practical answer for some people with severe learning disabilities who regularly try to masturbate in public. These people may need support to have the opportunity to masturbate in private.

Socio-cultural factors and religious beliefs

People with learning disabilities who may be aware of the expectations of others are the major focus of this section. Some people with learning disabilities, particularly those with a profound learning disability, will lack the cognitive understanding to be aware of other people's opinions on how they should conduct their sexual lives. However, the response to any sexual experiences they have, including masturbation and being sexually abused, will be governed largely by the values of those around them.

Gender expectations in relationships

Some people with learning disabilities are aware of certain social expectations for women and men regarding sex and relationships. Their learning disability may make it harder for them to challenge traditional ideas or to learn about other valued ways to be a man or a woman.

Research has shown that many women with learning disabilities believe:

- to be valued it is necessary to have a boyfriend or get married
- sex is something that women have to do to get or keep a boyfriend
- sex is something that men enjoy
- sex is not something that women should necessarily expect to enjoy.

These beliefs can make women with learning disabilities very vulnerable in their sexual relationships with men (McCarthy, 2009).

Similarly, research has found that men with learning disabilities often believe:

- having a girlfriend or getting married is a good thing
- having a boyfriend or sex with men is not a good thing
- girlfriends should let their boyfriends have sex with them
- sex is something that men enjoy.

These beliefs do not help men with learning disabilities to be sensitive partners in their relationships with women. It also can make them very vulnerable if they have sexual relationships with other men.

Good sex education or support on sexual issues should challenge such beliefs.

Same sex relationships and sexual identity

People with learning disabilities are likely to absorb messages from society that heterosexuality is the norm. They may also be less able than other people to question any messages they get that homosexuality is bad. This may cause those people who are interested in people of the same sex to feel guilty and hide their feelings.

The report *Secret Loves, Hidden Lives?* is an important piece of research that looked at the experiences of lesbians and gay men with learning disabilities (Abbott & Howarth, 2005). It found that many people had been physically or verbally abused because of their sexuality. Negative statements had come from a range of people including family and staff. It showed that to 'come out', people with learning disabilities can face greater obstacles than the rest of society. For example, it can be very difficult to have a private life that is not under the scrutiny of family or paid carers. Similarly, they may not be able to escape the prejudices of some people who are paid to support them.

Mental capacity

There are two main ways in which the level of a person's learning disability can have a direct impact on sex.

The first is the person's ability to understand sexual issues. This may include:

- their own body and its potential for sexual pleasure
- other people's bodies and what might be sexually pleasurable for them
- the motives of people who want to have sex with them
- the complexities of having relationships
- the challenges of raising children
- the laws about sex and consent
- the risk of STIs and what action can be taken to reduce the risks.

The second is how the person's life opportunities may be restricted in a way that is rare among people without a learning disability. Many people with learning disabilities are under almost constant supervision by family or staff. This can limit opportunities to:

- masturbate
- access, keep and use pornographic materials
- develop a relationship with another person, including having the opportunity to meet a person in private
- have sex with another person
- confide in other people about personal and sexual matters.

The support people get from their families and services will determine which of these things are available to them. On the whole, for good reason, the lives of most people with a profound learning disability are supervised and controlled. The implication for some of them is that they will be unable to decide to be alone or to masturbate because of physical disabilities. More able people with learning disabilities may have many more opportunities to make such decisions about their personal lives. Carers can have considerable control over the sexual lives of people with learning disabilities. The level of control will depend on the level of the person's learning disability. The values and knowledge of individual carers and services also play a big part.

The potential benefits of people with learning disabilities making decisions away from carers need to be considered alongside the risks, including the risk of sexual exploitation.

Understanding complex sexual issues

This section considers how mental capacity can impact on sexual issues. It suggests that some aspects of sexuality require a level of cognitive ability that is unavailable to some people with learning disabilities.

For example, when many people masturbate they fantasise about people they would like to be having sex with and/or doing specific sexual acts with. This is a complex thought process that may be impossible for people with more severe learning disabilities.

Similarly, people may use pornography when they masturbate. This may not be an option for some people with learning disabilities because they lack the cognitive skills to understand what is in the picture, or to relate it to sexual feelings.

Sexual orientation and identity

It can be argued that to be sexually interested in one gender over another requires knowledge of both genders. It may also require an ability to identify whether people are female or male. These are abilities that some people with learning disabilities will not have, although some people argue that sexual attraction is instinctive and does not require cognitive ability.

It may also be the case that some people with learning disabilities are less aware of the common assumption that a person is heterosexual rather than homosexual. This may be due to their difficulty in learning about social norms and values. Potentially, this may mean that the gender of the person they are having sex with is less important for some people with learning disabilities compared to people in the wider population. For this reason we need to be careful about imposing ideas of sexual orientation on people with learning disabilities. This means, for example, saying a person with severe learning disabilities is heterosexual when the person does not understand what that means.

Defining one's own sexual identity – whether it is heterosexual, bisexual, lesbian or gay – is abstract and so may be a difficult cognitive task for some people. It is also something that only an individual can do themselves.

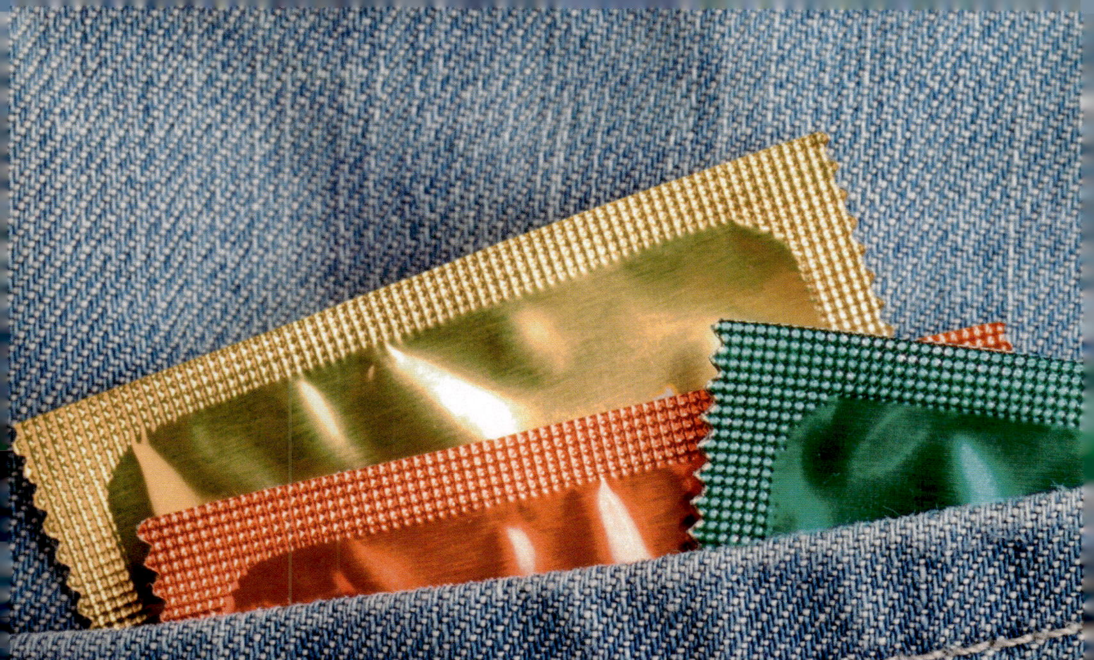

Section 3

Issues of sexual health and how these can be supported

Introduction

This section looks at how best to support people with sexual issues. It looks at what information people with learning disabilities may need about their bodies, relationships and sex if they are to have healthy sexual lives. It also looks at some common areas of concern, including masturbation, sexual abuse, pornography and the risk of sexually transmitted infections.

The key features of sexual health and well-being

Look again the World Health Organization's definition of sexual health on page 8.

Having knowledge about bodies and sex is vital for sexual health. Many people with learning disabilities have not been given information about their bodies and sex, which is a risk to their sexual health and well-being.

Sex education

The availability of sex education for people with learning disabilities is inconsistent. While sex education is part of the national curriculum in schools, it is unlikely to prepare people with learning disabilities for their sexual lives. This may be because it was provided at a level that the person could not understand or because it didn't cover situations relevant to the person's life.

When supporting a person with learning disabilities on sexual issues, do not assume that they have any sexual knowledge without first checking with them. Most people with learning disabilities, like other people, do not learn about sex at one time. They will get information from lots of different places and also learn from experience. Some of this information will be conflicting. For example, a person with learning disabilities might be told that sex is dirty and wrong by some people, and told that it is a pleasurable experience by others.

What to teach

When providing sex education to individuals or groups it is always a good idea to think about the most important things people need to know about bodies and sex. Try to teach these subjects before covering areas that might be irrelevant to the person's life at the time. For example, a young man with autism who shows little interest in relationships may have little need to learn about female bodies and periods. Similarly, it is very unlikely that knowing how babies are conceived, develop and are born will be relevant to the sexual lives of many people with learning disabilities. Knowing the reasons why people with learning disabilities rarely have children is likely to be more relevant to those who say they want children.

Sexual health issues that differently affect men and women

There are some differences in sexual health for men and women because their bodies and sexual possibilities are different. These differences include:

- periods
- menopause
- problems with erection and ejaculation in men
- problems with arousal and orgasm in women
- contraception including depot injections and the pill
- screening for gender-specific cancers.

There are also some issues that affect one gender more than the other. The main ones affecting people with learning disabilities are given below.

Females

- Poor body image
- Not getting pleasure from masturbation
- Desire to have children
- Lack of pleasure in sex with a male partner
- Tolerating being treated badly/ abused in a relationship because of concerns about losing the relationship

Males

- Exposure and masturbation in front of other people
- Inappropriate and abusive touching of other people
- Use of pornography
- Unmet desires of wanting sex
- Sexual contact or desire for sexual contact with people of the same sex

Supporting sexual health issues within plans for healthcare

This section looks at some of the most common issues and sets out possible plans. Where possible, involve other people in developing sexual healthcare plans. Depending on where you work this may mean involving a community nurse for people with learning disabilities or a psychologist.

Health action plans

Support for sexual issues should be included in health action plans. These are personal plans setting out what is needed to promote the health of people with learning disabilities. It is expected that every person with learning disabilities in England has a health action plan (DH, 2008).

Within health action plans, examples of actions related to sexual health may include:

- sex education or counselling
- support to attend a sexually transmitted disease clinic
- training for staff about responding to inappropriate sexual behaviour
- support for a PAP smear.

Masturbation

A careful assessment of the reasons why a person might have difficulty masturbating may lead to the following:

- referral to a specialist if there are problems with sexual development
- reviewing medication
- getting advice from an organisation for a particular syndrome
- giving a person private time without clothing or an incontinence pad that restricts masturbation.

If it is thought that the problem is with the person's technique, the following are options for a sexual healthcare plan:

- an education film showing masturbation
- showing possible techniques using a model penis or vagina

- providing lubrication, especially to men who have been circumcised
- providing a vibrator and suggestions about how it can be used.

Public masturbation

A health care plan should identify when and where a person can masturbate. For example, in the person's bedroom or bathroom, in a toilet cubicle at school or in another public building. As much as possible this should be communicated to the person. This may involve an exercise that asks the person whether certain places are good or bad places to masturbate. For some people it may mean physically taking them to an appropriate place if they start masturbating in public.

Where a person has some understanding of good and bad places to masturbate, it is very reasonable to try to communicate how serious it is if they continue to masturbate in public.

People with more severe learning disabilities may not be able to understand the seriousness of their behaviour. The following are management options that could be in a person's best interests:

- distraction techniques; some people masturbate at times because it is more interesting than the other options available – it may be necessary to offer other activities
- choosing clothing that makes it difficult for a person to touch their genitals when in public
- removing objects that cause arousal.

Pornography

Generally, a person's use of pornography should be accepted, unless the images are illegal. However, a care plan may include the following:

- keeping the material somewhere private
- not exposing other people, including staff and other service users to the images
- helping the person to understand that the pornography is unlikely to reflect any sex they have
- helping to understand feminists' concerns about pornography, ie. it presents women as objects for men's pleasure.

Keep in mind that it would be very difficult for services to justify accessing pornography on behalf of service users.

Inappropriate touch and sexual abusing

Care plans for people who sexually abuse may involve some of the following points. Much will depend on the assessment of the person's capacity to take responsibility for their behaviour.

- Setting out clearly what will happen if there is any future abusive behaviour.
- Education to help them understand the seriousness of their behaviour and how it may affect the people they abuse.
- Stopping access to, or increasing supervision when they are with, vulnerable people.

- Changing staffing arrangements, for example, only being supported by male staff if a man's abuse is directed at female staff.
- Putting restrictions on the person going out alone. This may be a deprivation of their liberty and so require legal safeguards. See the Deprivation of Liberty Safeguards (part of the Mental Capacity Act, 2005) on page 36.

It is sometimes suggested that the way to stop someone from sexually abusing is to help them get a partner. The research on men who abuse does not generally support this, nor does it recognise the vulnerability of their partner to sexual abuse.

Any suggestion of sexual suppressant medication should also be resisted. This is because there is almost no evidence that it is effective with men with learning disabilities.

Sex between women and men

Where there is a sexual relationship between two people with learning disabilities, the support offered as part of a sexual healthcare plan could include:

- helping a person with learning disabilities who is being taken advantage of sexually to recognise how unfair this is and what their choices are
- challenging the behaviour of someone who is taking advantage of the other person
- assertiveness in relationships
- giving women and men information about women's bodies and women's potential for sexual pleasure
- giving information about the possibility of pregnancy and contraception
- assessing a woman's capacity to make a decision about pregnancy and making a best interests decision about what needs to happen if she lacks capacity
- supporting women to access contraception
- giving information about sexually transmitted diseases
- supporting individuals to be checked for sexually transmitted diseases and to access preventative treatments, for example, a hepatitis B vaccination
- countering any resistance to a person with learning disabilities having a sexual relationship, for example, from paid carers
- facilitating the opportunity to have sex in an appropriate and respectful place; too many people with learning disabilities are prevented from having private time in their bedrooms
- providing information about marriage and support for this to happen.

Same sex relationships

Support for people involved in same sex relationships could cover:

- understanding that sex and relationships between people of the same sex can be a positive thing
- helping a person with learning disabilities who is being taken advantage of sexually to recognise how unfair this is and what their choices are

Case example

Staff members find a woman and man with learning disabilities engaging in sexual contact in a toilet cubicle at college. They are both very distressed to have been found and think that they have done something wrong. They are known to have been a couple for several years. While there is some concern about their sexual knowledge, there are no concerns that either is being abused. The man lives in his own flat with staff coming in and the woman lives in a group home with 24-hour staffing. The man visits his girlfriend at the group home but has been told by staff that they cannot be alone in her bedroom.

What support would you offer the couple?

- challenging the behaviour of men who are taking advantage of the other person
- giving information about sexual activities and what may or may not be pleasurable
- giving information about sexually transmitted diseases, particularly to men where there is anal penetration, including HIV/Aids and HIV testing
- practical skills for men using condoms; this would include putting them on if they penetrate other men, or how to encourage other men to use them if they are penetrated
- supporting individuals, particularly men, to be checked for sexually transmitted diseases and to access preventative treatments
- assessing a man's capacity to consent to HIV testing and whether they lack capacity to make a best interests decision about this considering the potential risk
- countering any resistance to a person with learning disabilities having a sexual relationship
- facilitating the opportunity to have sex in an appropriate and respectful place

Thinking activity

Why is it important to balance showing sex education resources depicting images of abuse with images of couples enjoying sex?

- providing information about civil partnerships and marriage and support for this to happen.

Thinking activity

If a woman with learning disabilities lacks capacity to consent to penetrative vaginal sex, could she be capable of making an informed decision about using contraception?

People who have been sexually abused

People who have been sexually abused can benefit from specialist support and advice (see Useful contacts on page 54).

Sexual health care plans with people who have been sexually abused can include:

- education to help the person understand why what was done to them was wrong
- reassurance that they have not done anything wrong themselves
- sexual health and pregnancy checks
- counselling or psychotherapy
- ensuring that the person is not exposed to an unacceptable risk of further abuse.

This work is particularly difficult with people with the most severe learning disabilities.

The most important element is their ongoing safety. This may mean, for example, removing the men with learning disabilities who have abused them from the services they share.

Contraception

A women's capacity to make a decision about using contraception should first be assessed. It is the responsibility of the prescribing doctor to make this decision, but it is helpful if other people who know her are also involved. Therefore, before a woman is taken to her GP to discuss contraception, individuals who know her well should explore her understanding of the following, and where possible provide her with information.

The discussion with the woman should cover:

- how babies are conceived
- any genetic reasons why she may have difficulty getting pregnant
- the possibility of her sexual activity (if any) leading to pregnancy
- the difference between consensual sex and abuse
- the challenges of raising children, including the risk that they will be taken away.

It may be unclear or there may be differing opinions regarding a woman's ability to make a decision about using contraception and extra support may resolve this. Where this does not happen it may be necessary to go to the Court of Protection to make a decision.

If a woman is able to make her own decision then this is what needs to happen, regardless of the concerns of others. It is, for example, not uncommon for women with learning disabilities who have had children taken away to want to have other children and so not use contraception. Under the Mental Capacity Act (2005) a woman's decision not to use contraception could be an unwise decision that needs to be accepted.

Contraception and men

Men with learning disabilities who may be having consensual sex with women could benefit from:

- information about how pregnancy can happen and be prevented
- an exploration of their views about having children and how realistic this could be
- information about any genetic condition they have which may reduce their fertility
- information about the options for women
- information about the options for men
- practical support about using condoms, including getting, opening, putting them on, and checking that they have not come off (model penises can be very helpful here).

However, unless the man is infertile or has chosen to be sterilised it would be very unwise to expect him to take full responsibility for contraception. Consistent condom use can be very challenging even when a man with learning disabilities is motivated to use them.

Sexually transmitted diseases

A challenge when working with people with learning disabilities who may be having sex is to provide information about STIs in a way that is relevant and helpful.

The basic information that people with learning disabilities who may be having sex could benefit from, includes:

- if you have sexual contact with another person you can get ill if you catch a sexually transmitted disease
- there are different types of diseases you can get

Thinking activity

How do people you know manage the risk of STIs?

- using condoms can help prevent diseases (assuming at least one partner is male).

If there are concerns that a person is at risk of getting an STI (or passing one on) this needs to be addressed with the individual. An assessment with an individual who may be at risk would need to look at:

- who they are having sex with
- any knowledge of the people they are having sex with having STIs
- how often the sex takes place
- what kind of sex takes place – some sexual acts are more risky than others
- any history of STIs.

A sexual health clinic could be of use when carrying out an assessment of risk.

Where a person with learning disabilities has been assessed as lacking capacity to make decisions about a significant risk of acquiring (or passing on) a sexually transmitted disease, decisions need to be made in their best interests. This could involve:

- providing further education
- screening for STDs including having regular checks
- HIV testing
- providing vaccinations, for example hepatitis B
- restricting opportunities for sex that puts them at risk.

The last point is controversial. It involves weighing up the potentially negative aspects of having a sexually transmitted disease with the impact of restrictions on a person's life.

Local services that support sexual health for individuals

Searching locally could identify professionals or services that are able to work directly with people with learning disabilities on sexual issues. Alternatively, you could find people who could advise you or your organisation about how to best support an individual. Sometimes it is helpful to find someone to provide training for a staff team so that they respond consistently and helpfully to the sexual health needs of clients.

There are limited numbers of people who have extensive experience and expertise in supporting people with learning disabilities on sexual issues. Therefore, it is often a good idea for those people who are confident talking about sexual issues to work in partnership with those who have a good understanding of the lives of people with learning disabilities. For example, you might work with a local lesbian and gay organisation to think about how best to support a woman with learning disabilities who identifies as a lesbian.

Possible services that you could call upon for support include:

- your organisation
- community teams for people with learning disabilities
- sexual health clinics (for information about local services go to NHS Choices – www.nhs.uk)
- contraception and pregnancy advice services (information can also be found on NHS choices or the FPA website (www.fpa.org.uk)

- sexual abuse/assault services
- lesbian, gay and transgender organisations. A good place to search for local organisations is the Turing Network (http://www.turingnetwork.org.uk/)
- health promotion services
- religious groups
- dating agencies (see Useful contacts).

Thinking activity

Identify where you could take a person with learning disabilities who has recently been sexually abused in order to collect forensic evidence. How might the person with learning disabilities feel about evidence being collected, and how could you support them?

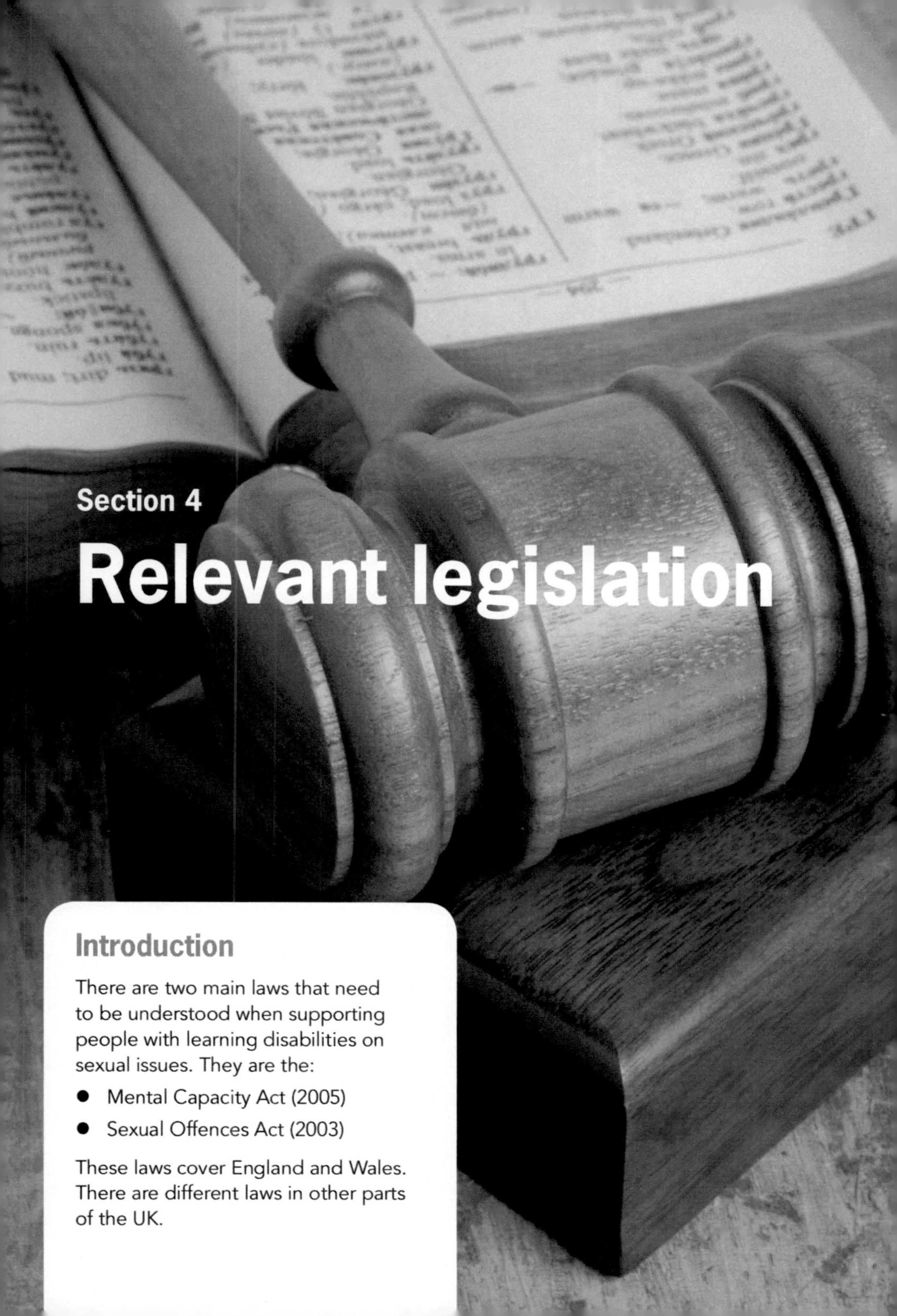

Section 4

Relevant legislation

Introduction

There are two main laws that need to be understood when supporting people with learning disabilities on sexual issues. They are the:

- Mental Capacity Act (2005)
- Sexual Offences Act (2003)

These laws cover England and Wales. There are different laws in other parts of the UK.

The Mental Capacity Act (2005)

The parents of children under the age of 16 have the legal power to make decisions for them. This includes decisions about how children with learning disabilities will be supported on sexual issues.

Thinking activity

How would you feel if someone else was deciding whether or not you could be alone with another adult in your bedroom?

The Mental Capacity Act (MCA) (2005) outlines how decisions must be made for people with learning disabilities who are 16 or over.

The MCA says we need to work with individuals over 16 in one of two ways:

- supporting them to make their own decisions
- making decisions in their best interests if they do not have capacity.

The MCA is all about decisions, including sexual decisions. For example:

- what to do if a person is having difficulty masturbating
- whether an adult can spend time with another adult in their bedroom
- whether a woman should use contraception
- what to do if a man is found using pornography
- what to do if you are worried that an adult is being taken advantage of sexually.

The MCA states that no one should be making decisions for people who can make their own decisions.

Thinking activity

Think about the last time you worked with a person with learning disabilities. What decisions were made during this time? Who made the decisions? Was it the person, staff or the person's family? If decisions were not made by the person, were they made in their best interests?

The five principles of the Mental Capacity Act and what they mean for sexual decisions

1. **The person must be assumed to have capacity unless it is established that they lack capacity.**
   Our starting point must be a belief that people with learning disabilities can have sex and relationships.

2. **A person is not to be treated as unable to make a decision unless all practical steps to help him to do so have been taken without success.**
   This principle recognises that support can help people to make decisions for themselves. It requires us to provide sex education to help individuals develop knowledge and skills. This should be done as much as possible before coming to the conclusion that the person cannot make a particular decision about sex.

3. **A person is not to be treated as unable to make a decision merely because he makes an unwise decision.**
   This principle reminds us that people are allowed to make what other people might consider to be bad decisions. For example, going out with someone who does not treat us well is a mistake we can all make. It does not mean we lack capacity to decide who we date.

4. **An act done, or decision made, under this act for or on behalf of a person who lacks capacity must be done, or made, in his best interests.**
   This principle has two requirements. The first is the need to assess someone as lacking capacity to make a decision before doing anything on their behalf. The second tells us that any action taken on the person's behalf must be in their best interests. Next, you will look at how to assess capacity and what needs to be thought about when deciding what is in a person's best interests.

- **Before the act is done, or the decision is made, regard has to be had to whether the purpose for which it is needed can be as effectively achieved in a way that is less restrictive of the person's rights and freedom of action.**
  When acting in a person's best interests we need to try to minimise the restrictions we place on the person. A common mistake is thinking that this means we must do what is least restrictive.

Thinking activity

A woman with learning disabilities is taken by her mother to get contraception from her GP. The mother explains her concern about the risk of pregnancy and controlling period pains.

What should the GP do?

The MCA and its principles are extremely helpful in working out how to respond to any sexual situation involving a person with learning disabilities. It sets out a clear structure for thinking. This is shown in Diagram 1 below.

There will often be disagreements about whether a person has capacity to make a particular decision, or what might be in a person's best interests. Both these areas will be looked at before finding out what should happen if people cannot agree.

Capacity to consent to sex

As part of the legal process there may be an assessment of a person's capacity to consent to sex. There may be slight differences between tests of capacity under the Sexual Offences Act (2003), which are done by courts, and those done under the Mental Capacity Act (2005), which are undertaken by professionals and carers.

When there is a chance that a person with learning disabilities has been involved in sexual contact a common question is whether they could consent to it. If a person has severe learning disabilities it might be very straightforward to say that they lack capacity to consent to sexual contact. Usually, it is much more difficult.

What people with learning disabilities need to know in order to consent to sex was tested in the Court of Protection (D Borough Council & AB [2011] EWHC 101 (COP)). The judge suggested that the only knowledge required was:

- the mechanics of the act
- that there are health risks involved, particularly the acquisition of sexually transmitted diseases and sexually transmissible infections

Diagram 1: Decision-making flowchart

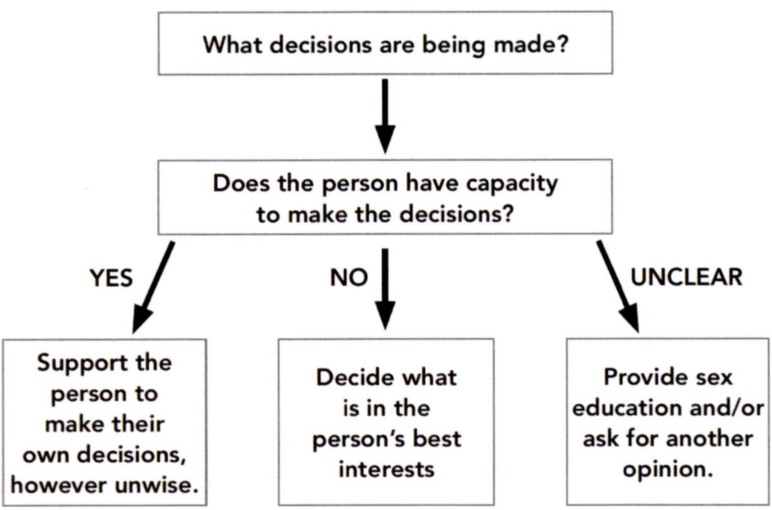

- that sex between a man and a woman may result in the woman becoming pregnant.

It is essential that people with learning disabilities have information about the emotional aspects of sex as well as some understanding of what constitutes abuse.

General and specific consent

Two aspects of capacity to consent to sex need to be considered – the general and specific.

1. Does the person have the capacity to make decisions about sex in general? ie. do they have enough understanding to be making their own decisions about who they have sex with and what sex they have?
2. Does the person have the capacity to consent specifically to the sexual contact they are likely to be having with particular individuals?

Individuals may have one form of capacity and not the other.

It is important to consider a person's ability to apply the information they have. This would include:

- the ability to say no to specific sexual activities
- the ability of a woman to get a male partner to use condoms to avoid an unwanted pregnancy or STDs
- the ability of a man to get a male partner to put a condom on to avoid STDs, including HIV.

When considering a person's ability to consent to sexual relationships, if it is known who they are having sex with it is possible to consider their capacity to make sexual decisions specifically with that person (or persons). Knowing the couple can potentially reduce the amount of information either person would require to be able to consent to sex. For example:

- if one partner in a heterosexual couple is infertile, the need for information and skills regarding contraception may not be relevant
- if there is sex between two men with learning disabilities that does not include anal sex, and neither is thought to have had sex (or be having sex) with other people, there is little need for information about condom use and HIV.

In the cases when it is not known who a person with learning disabilities might be having sex with, it will often be with men who do not have learning disabilities. In such situations it is reasonable to assume that the person with learning disabilities, whether female or male, will find it difficult to make choices about what sexual activities take place, or to insist that the man uses condoms. At best they may be able to resist particular sexual activities.

Best interests decisions

If a person has been assessed as lacking capacity to make a decision, the decision needs to be made for them in their best interests. The service providing support to the individual must decide what is in the person's best interests For example:

- a day service deciding whether they should let two people spend time together

- a group home deciding whether to always supervise a person when they are out
- a doctor deciding whether to prescribe contraception.

The only exceptions to this are if the person has a health and welfare attorney or a deputy who has the power to make the specific decision. Alternatively, the Court of Protection can make decisions about what is in a person's best interests.

Families supporting their relative with learning disabilities will usually be making decisions in their best interests. However, unlike people paid to support people with learning disabilities, they are not required to comply with the MCA.

The MCA says that one best interests decision that cannot be made is to give consent for someone to have sex. This is one of a number of 'excluded decisions': decisions that cannot be made on behalf of people who lack capacity to make them themselves.

This also excludes arranging for a prostitute to have sex with a person who lacks capacity to consent to paid-for sex.

People can make the mistake of thinking that this excluded decision means that services cannot make any decisions about what to do if a person lacking capacity to consent may be having sex. They may believe that the only response is to do everything possible to stop the possibility of sex happening. This is wrong, because the MCA requires us to do what is in the person's best interests. Sometimes this will be to take action to stop the possibility of sex happening. However, sometimes it will be in the person's best interests to allow that possibility, even if the sex might be sexual abuse.

Best interests checklist

The MCA provides a list of things that have to be thought about when making best interests decisions.

1. **The person's views and wishes**
   Even if a person has been assessed as lacking capacity to make a decision, we still need to pay attention to their wishes. As much as possible, best interests decisions should reflect the individual's views and wishes. If it does go against the person's views, it may be necessary to take the decision to the Court of Protection – particularly for the most able people with learning disabilities.

Thinking activity

What are the other excluded decisions in the Mental Capacity Act?

2. **The views of people who know the person well**
   When making best interests decisions there is an expectation that people who know the person best are involved in the decision. The people to be consulted include family members who have an ongoing relationship with the individual. Friends should also be considered. Usually, more than one family member or friend will need to be involved. Staff members who have a good understanding of the person's needs should also be included. In many cases they will be frontline staff and not managers.

   If a person is living in the family home, services should be very careful about overriding the views of the family about what is in the person's best interests. Where there is a serious concern that a family is not acting in a person's best interests, the local authority should take these concerns to the Court of Protection.
3. **Consider all relevant information**
   In addition to the views of the person and those who are consulted, other information will need to be considered. This may include information about:
   - the person's learning disability and needs
   - previous sexual behaviour and the consequences of this
   - the person's living situation and support
   - the possibility of the person receiving sex education, which may lead them to have capacity to make the decision themselves
   - the possible effectiveness of different options, possibly using research evidence
   - the cost of different options.
4. **Try to limit restrictions on the person's rights and freedom**
   The fifth principle of the MCA requires us to think about options that would limit restrictions on the person. It does not require us to always choose the less restrictive option. This is because the less restrictive option may not be in the person's best interests or it may be unaffordable.

   The MCA code of practice is very clear that best interests decisions can involve the use of restrictions and restraint. For example, it may be in a person's best interests to:
   - physically move the person's hand away from their genital area if they are trying to masturbate in public
   - use clothes that restrict a person's ability to masturbate in public
   - secure the door to the person's home to prevent them behaving sexually inappropriately in public
   - exclude a person from a day centre to prevent them sexually abusing other service users
   - prescribe a woman with learning disabilities contraception even though she wishes to have children (this decision may need to be taken to the Court of Protection).

The Court of Protection

Decisions that may need to be taken to the Court of Protection include disagreements about:

- whether a person has capacity to consent to sex
- whether it is in the best interests of a woman to use contraception when she expresses a wish to have children
- whether it is in someone's best interests to restrict their freedom to reduce the risk of them sexually abusing other people
- whether it is in someone's best interests to restrict their freedom to reduce the risk of being sexually abused
- whether it is in the best interests of a man to restrict his freedom to reduce the risk of acquiring or passing on HIV.

There does not always have to be a disagreement for cases to go to the Court of Protection. The Court of Protection *must* be involved when:

- sterilising a woman or man who lacks capacity to make this decision
- removing a woman from the family home because of a risk of sexual abuse, against the family's wishes.

This is because doctors or local authority safeguarding teams do not have the legal power to make these decisions.

Deprivation of Liberty Safeguards

The Deprivation of Liberty Safeguards (DoLS) are part of the MCA. They can give extra protection to adults when best interests decisions are made to use restraint or restrictions. The safeguards are there to make sure that what is being done is in the person's best interests.

The DoLS can only be used if the person is in a care home or hospital. If someone is living in a care home, the following are examples of when the DoLS should be used for sexual situations.

- A man has often gone out without staff, but because of the risk of his sexual behaviour it is decided that he now needs to be always escorted by staff.
- A woman is used to going out without staff, but after being sexually abused it is decided that it is unsafe for her go out alone.

Using the DoLS, someone independent would check that the person lacked capacity to decide about going out alone, and whether it was in their best interests to only go out with staff. If either of the examples involved people in supported living, it would be the Court of Protection that would need to make the decision.

If the person was living in the family home they could stop the person going out without needing to get anyone's permission. The local authority would have no power to stop the family doing this, even as part of adult safeguarding. However, if the local authority was concerned that what was happening went against the person's best interests then they could go to the Court of Protection.

In both examples it is about putting restrictions on people who are used to going out by themselves. It is very unlikely that the DoLS would be needed in care homes for people with learning disabilities who have never been able to go out alone because of the risk of traffic or getting lost.

Thinking activity

What information should be shared in each of the three situations listed on this page?

Confidentiality and the MCA

People often want to keep information about their sexual lives private. The Data Protection Act (DPA) (1998, 2003) supports people's privacy by putting limits on what information can be held and shared by organisations. The following examples are common dilemmas concerning the DPA.

1. A person tells a staff member about a relationship that sounds exploitative and abusive. They do not want the staff member to tell anyone else about it.
2. A man with learning disabilities has abused other service users. As a consequence he is moved to a different service. It is suggested that information about what he has done should not be shared with the new service because of the DPA.
3. A man and woman with learning disabilities have started a sexual relationship. It is suggested that the woman's parents are not told about this because of a concern that they would take action to stop it.

The Mental Capacity Act (2005) should inform what happens in each of the situations previously listed. The first question to ask is: does the person have capacity to make the decision about what is shared, or can they be supported to be able to make that decision? This may be the case in the third example. Where a person has been assessed as lacking capacity to make a decision, information may be shared legally if it is believed to be in their best interests.

The Sexual Offences Act (2003)

The Sexual Offences Act (2003) identifies sexual crimes. People with learning disabilities are often the victims of sexual crimes. Some people with learning disabilities, particularly men, may also commit sexual crimes.

Both adults and children with learning disabilities are covered by the act. There are also extra offences that recognise that some people are particularly vulnerable to being sexually exploited. In the act these are called 'offences against people with mental disorder'. This includes people with learning disabilities and those with particular mental health problems.

General offences

The sexual offences listed in the table below apply to everyone.

Other general sexual offences include exposure, voyeurism and making someone have sex with another person. These also require a lack of consent.

Consent is defined in the Sexual Offences Act as: 'A person consents if he agrees by choice and has the freedom and capacity to make that choice.' (Section 74)

Any sex involving a child under 16 can be an offence, although the law recognises that some children who are 13 and over can consent to sex. Where this is found, prosecution is unlikely provided that the other person is under 18.

It is very unlikely that any child with learning disabilities between the ages of 13 and 16 would have the capacity to consent to sex. For this reason, sex education for young people with learning disabilities can be simplified to 'no one is allowed to have sex under 16'.

Offences against people with mental disorder

There are three sets of offences that provide additional protection for people with mental disorders including learning disabilities. They cover sex with a person, making the person have sex with other people, and exposing them to sexual activity.

Offences against persons with mental disorder impeding choice

The law recognises that people with learning disabilities may lack capacity to choose whether to agree to

General offences under the Sexual Offences Act (2003)	
Rape	The intentional penetration with a penis of the vagina, anus or mouth of another person, without that person's consent. Rape has automatically been committed when penetration occurs with a child under the age of 13. Rape is the only sexual offence that can only be committed by a man.
Assault by penetration	The intentional penetration of the vagina or anus by males or females with a part of the body, an object, or anything else.
Sexual assault	Any kind of intentional sexual touching of someone else without their consent. It includes touching (sexually) any part of their body, clothed or unclothed, either with any part of the body or with an object.

sexual activity with some people because either:

- they lack sufficient understanding of the nature or reasonably foreseeable consequences of the sexual activity, or for any other reason
- they are unable to communicate their choice.

Guilt is dependent on the potential perpetrator knowing, or it is reasonable to expect them to know, that the person has a mental disorder, and that they are therefore unlikely to be able to refuse.

Inducements, threats and deception

The vulnerability of people with learning disabilities to agree to sex because of what they are told will happen if they either agree or disagree is also recognised. Again, to prove guilt the potential perpetrator needs to know, or could reasonably be expected to know, that the person has learning disabilities.

Examples of inducements could include giving gifts, including money, or promising to be their boyfriend. Deception could be telling lies such as, 'All your friends do this' or 'You'll get ill if you don't'. Threats might include 'I'll tell your parents' or 'I'll hurt your friend'.

Sexual offences involving care workers

The law is clear that staff must not have sex with people with learning disabilities. The maximum penalty is 10 years in prison. It applies to anyone in regular face-to-face contact with and providing services to people with learning disabilities.

Care workers include people working for the NHS, social services, private and voluntary agencies and also volunteers. As well as more obvious staff, such as day centre and residential workers, it also includes people like therapists, cleaners, taxi drivers, gardeners and caretakers.

Thinking activity

Think of a person with learning disabilities you know who is able to go out by themselves. Make a list of all roles of workers who have regular face-to-face contact with them. Include any volunteers in this list of people covered in the sexual offences involving care workers. How would you explain to people with learning disabilities the reasons why they cannot have relationships with these people?

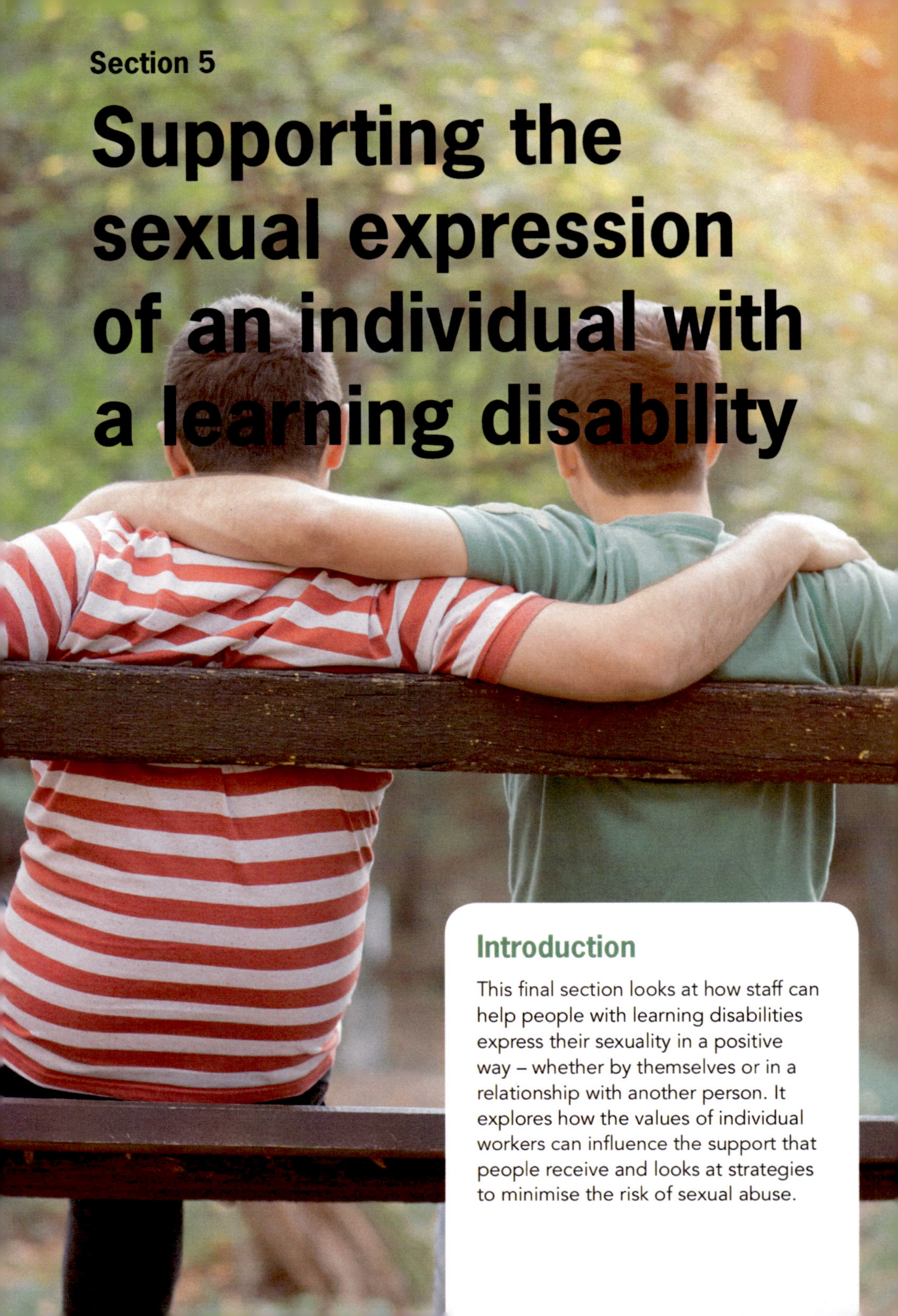

Section 5

Supporting the sexual expression of an individual with a learning disability

Introduction

This final section looks at how staff can help people with learning disabilities express their sexuality in a positive way – whether by themselves or in a relationship with another person. It explores how the values of individual workers can influence the support that people receive and looks at strategies to minimise the risk of sexual abuse.

How a carer's values, belief systems and experiences may impact on support

Carers' beliefs will be shaped by social-cultural values, including their religious beliefs. These will be about sexual issues in general, as well as specifically in relation to people with learning disabilities. This means that your values will influence how you support people.

Thinking activity

Identify examples of a person with learning disabilities receiving good and poor support on sexual issues. What values of the carers will have influenced the support (or lack of it)?

Ann Craft pioneered supporting people with learning disabilities on sexual issues in the UK and set out the following charter of rights.

1. The right to grow up, that is, to be treated with the respect and dignity accorded to adults.
2. The right to know, that is, to have access and assimilate information about themselves, their bodies and those of other people, their emotions, and appropriate social behaviour.
3. The right to be sexual and to make and break relationships.
4. The right not to be at the mercy of the individual sexual attitudes of different caregivers.
5. The right not to be sexually abused.
6. The right to humane and dignified environments.

(Craft, 1987)

The following examples are some of the values and belief systems that may influence work on sexual issues with people with learning disabilities.

- Is masturbation a good thing?
- Are same sex relationships of equal value as opposite sex relationships?
- Should sex only take place in a committed relationship?
- Should people with learning disabilities have children?
- Should sex only be about having children?
- Is contraception acceptable?
- Is pornography acceptable?

It is impossible not to have your own views and when working with people with learning disabilities it is important to be aware of what your personal values are and the influence they might have. This is particularly the case if you share them with the people you support.

When providing sexual support it will always be acceptable to share the values of society that are relevant to the person's needs. This is what is and is not allowed by law.

Thinking activity

Read the list of questions on page 41 and consider your values. Does it make a difference if the people involved have learning disabilities?

Religion

Religion can play a big part in some people's values and what is expected of them. This includes staff and people with learning disabilities.

The following examples illustrate two situations where there could be a conflict with religious values.

1. The religious values of the person with learning disabilities and/or their family conflicting with the values of the service.
2. The religious values of a staff member conflicting with the values of a person with learning disabilities or the service.

Care needs to be taken when discussing religious values so that assumptions are not made about what they are. It is important to remember that in every religion there is a diversity of views.

It should be unacceptable for staff to share religious beliefs that are against UK law. This includes expressing such beliefs in words or actions. For example, the following will always be unacceptable for staff in a work setting.

- Stopping someone from masturbating because their religion tells them it is wrong.
- Telling someone that their religion says that having sex before marriage is wrong.

The two examples would put individuals at the mercy of the individual sexual attitudes of caregivers – something that Ann Craft campaigned against.

Meaningful relationships and the development of an individual's sexuality

For people with learning disabilities, having an ongoing relationship can have the following benefits for their sexuality:

- companionship, intimacy and love
- increased self-esteem
- enjoying sex.

It is important to remember that people with learning disabilities may not be able to recognise that they are being treated badly and lack the ability to challenge this. Other general differences are that having children and looking after children are unlikely in relationships involving people with learning disabilities. People with learning disabilities may also be particularly vulnerable to financial exploitation. When supporting people with learning disabilities in relationships it is unwise to assume that both partners will be enjoying sex. Ideally, both individuals will be offered the opportunity to talk about their relationship, including sex. An aim of this is to try to ensure that they understand the following:

- what things people often do when they have sex: oral, anal and vaginal
- sex should feel nice for both people
- you do not have to do anything you do not want to
- you should not make anyone do something they do not want to
- what could help sex feel nicer, for example, using lubricants or stimulating the clitoris.

Ways an individual can express themselves sexually and how this can be supported

This guide has already given lots of examples about how people can be supported to express themselves sexually and how individual preferences can be supported, including:

- supporting people to masturbate in private
- providing sex education
- communicating the acceptability of same sex relationships
- accessing sexual health services.

The following are common signs of a service not offering this support:

- making rules that it is unacceptable to masturbate in private at any time when a person is at a particular service – for example, a school or day centre
- giving people single beds rather than the choice of a double bed (the preference of most adults)
- making arbitrary rules about people not being able to have anyone in their bedrooms or to stay over at night
- not providing opportunities for people to talk intimately about sex.

It is important to think about what support might be provided to a person with learning disabilities who wants one of the following:

- a girlfriend or boyfriend
- sex
- children.

Wanting a girlfriend or boyfriend

Wanting a relationship is a desire shared by many people. There are some common challenges when people with learning disabilities want a relationship.

This includes wanting to go out with a celebrity or a staff member. As it is against the law for staff members to go out with people with learning disabilities, it is relatively easy to get around this issue by explaining that staff are not allowed to go out with people with learning disabilities. Similarly, individuals might wish to have a relationship with people without learning disabilities who they know in their local community. Often, people's hopes are humoured or even encouraged by the responses they get. The alternative of explaining that such people would not go out with them because of their learning disability is very painful, so it is often avoided.

Meeting other people with learning disabilities

The best opportunity for people with learning disabilities to have an ongoing relationship where they will not be exploited is with other people with learning disabilities. This is likely to be with those they share a service with, for example, a residential service, college, day centre or social club.

Moving away from special settings for people with learning disabilities can reduce opportunities for meeting potential partners. Too often, people with learning disabilities lose touch with those they have shared large parts of their lives with (who may already be boyfriends or girlfriends) when they leave a service or when it closes. This may because:

- they may lack the skills and opportunities to maintain contact
- they may lack the support of the service to maintain relationships
- staff often do not know who a person's friends are, or do not help them spend time together outside shared services.

To promote opportunities for people with learning disabilities to have friends and intimate relationships, services need to help people to:

- keep an address book; it is useful to include how best to get in touch with their friends and any support they might need to meet
- to get contact details of those people they would like to stay in touch with when they leave a service
- make arrangements to meet friends and relationships outside the services they share
- tell friends their new address if they have moved
- access social opportunities with other people with learning disabilities.

Dating and friendship agencies for people with learning disabilities could also be an option.

Being able to have private time

For those people with learning disabilities who have a boyfriend or girlfriend, having the chance to spend private time together can be very difficult. The message from many services is that this is not allowed. For this reason, people with learning disabilities often have to grab intimacy when they can, in places that are the best available to them, but often undesirable.

If people with learning disabilities want to spend time together alone, or are found alone together, this needs to be respected if both partners have the capacity to make this decision. This should allow, for example, people to have partners in their bedrooms, including staying overnight. Where one person lacks capacity to make the decision, services need to think about what is in their best interests under the Mental Capacity Act (2005).

Wanting sex

Some men with learning disabilities may express a desire to have sex. Occasionally carers may think that a man with learning disabilities could benefit from a sexual relationship. Rarely do these things apply to women.

Generally, if a man is expressing a wish to have sex, he may need help to understand the difficulties he might have in achieving this, as well as the requirement of consent. Support could also be directed at helping develop a relationship where sex may become a possibility. However, care must be taken not to expose vulnerable people with learning disabilities to a man who, in his desire to have sex, may pay little attention to their wishes or experience.

The harsh reality for many men with learning disabilities who want sex is that they may not have the opportunity to have a sexual relationship in their life. This may be because they have physical problems, lack skills to develop or have few opportunities for a relationship, or are seen as an unattractive partner. Sensitive support would respect that this could be difficult for men.

Supporting an individual to keep safe

It is useful to be aware of the groups that are most likely to abuse people with learning disabilities. The starting point is to recognise that in the vast majority of cases the perpetrators will be men. This gives good reason to be particularly careful of the contact any men have with both women and men with learning disabilities. This, of course, does not deny the possibility of women sexually abusing.

Research shows that the most likely abusers are:

- men with learning disabilities using the same services
- male carers
- male family members.

The least likely group was found to be strangers (Brown *et al*, 1995; McCarthy & Thompson, 1997) as many people with learning disabilities are supervised continuously by family members or paid carers, reducing the chance of a stranger being in contact with them.

Giving people information to protect themselves

A person's level of learning disability will influence how effective sex education is in protecting the individual from abuse. Sex education should cover the following:

- the difference between consensual and non-consensual sex
- knowing that it is against the law for care workers and family members to have sex with people with learning disabilities
- the right to say no if you do not want to have sex with someone or to do specific sexual activities
- an awareness of sexual exploitation, for example, people being tricked into having sex, or men making promises that they will not keep
- what to do and who to tell if you are being sexually exploited or abused

- who has done something wrong when there is sexual abuse; this is important because some people with learning disabilities think they have done something wrong if they have any sex, including if they have been sexually abused.

A common outcome of providing sex education to people with learning disabilities is for individuals to speak about abuse that has happened or is happening. This is because sex education can give people permission to communicate sexual things – this could be in words or gestures.

Providing information for protection should not be a one-off event but people should have opportunities to reinforce their learning throughout their lives.

Fundamental to people being able to protect themselves from abuse, and to let people know if it has happened, is having a sense of self-worth or rights. This may be a belief that bad things should not happen to them, and if they do something will be done about it.

Thinking activity

Try to simplify the list on page 45 on what sex education should cover into one or two statements that would be good for people with learning disabilities to know and remember.

Avoiding people being put in vulnerable situations

Shared residential services, independent living, being with or without staff in community settings, and day and social facilities expose people to different sexual risks. The following may increase the probability of people being sexually abused:

- People having to share services with more able men with learning disabilities, including men with histories of sexually abusing.
- Inadequate screening of staff, including CRB checks.
- Male staff providing intimate care to women or providing support to women in their homes when there are no other staff present. This situation can also make male staff very vulnerable because of the possibility of allegations of abuse.
- People living alone with limited support, family contact or activities. Our knowledge of disability hate crime shows how often these people may be exploited in various ways.

Being alert to the possibility of sexual abuse

Potential signs of abuse include:

- people having a knowledge about sex that is surprising for their level of learning disability

- unexplained incontinence, soiling or blood on bedding or clothing
- unexplained wounds to the vagina or anus, or other injuries like bruising
- sexually transmitted diseases or pregnancy
- people becoming withdrawn or upset
- someone talking about a relationship with a man who is unknown to and avoids contact with carers
- a person receiving gifts or money that may indicate sexual exploitation
- a person being unexpectedly short of money; sexual abuse may accompany financial abuse.

An aspect of being aware of the possibility of abuse is developing relationships with the people you work with so that they would feel able to tell you if something was wrong or was worrying them.

Thinking activity

What attributes can staff have that might make it more and less likely that people with learning disabilities will talk to them about personal things?

Taking action when sexual abuse has taken place

A good response to possible sexual abuse is to provide support that helps people make sense of what has happened to them as well as practical interventions. This may include the following:

- urgent contact with the police so that evidence can be collected
- counselling and therapy
- support to move away from an abusive environment
- support with giving evidence and appearing in court.

There are excellent examples of therapeutic work being offered to people with severe learning disabilities who have been sexually abused (see Respond in Useful contacts). Work with individuals may help them challenge any future sexual abuse or exploitation in relationships.

Prosecuting abusers would be a good response although this often doesn't happen, perhaps because of the police's unwillingness to intervene, a lack of evidence, or concern for the individual about going through the legal process.

Other protective strategies should also be considered.

- Seeing whether there may be other vulnerable people who may have been abused by the same perpetrator.

- Sacking staff members who may have abused people with learning disabilities, even if there is insufficient evidence for a legal prosecution. These staff should be reported to the Independent Safeguarding Authority.
- Moving and/or increasing the supervision of men with learning disabilities who have sexually abused others.

Local authority safeguarding adults procedures

If anyone suspects that a person with learning disabilities is being sexually abused it must be reported to the local authority's safeguarding adult team. If it involves a child, child protection services must be involved.

All decisions made as part of adult safeguarding teams must comply with the Mental Capacity Act (2005). This means that where possible the person who may be being abused is making their own decisions about what should happen, for example, ending a relationship, deciding to involve the police or whether to move or not. If the person is found to lack capacity to make any of these decisions, best interests decisions must be made (see page 33).

Thinking activity

Think about a person with learning disabilities you have had recent contact with.

Where might the risk of sexual abuse come from?

What is in place currently to reduce the risk of them being sexually abused?

What further action could be taken to increase their protection from abuse?

References

Abbott D & Howarth J (2005) *Secret Loves, Hidden Lives: Exploring issues for people with learning difficulties who are gay, lesbian or bisexual*. Bristol: The Policy Press.

Brown H, Stein J & Turk V (1995) The sexual abuse of adults with learning disabilities: a report of a second two-year incidence survey. *Mental Handicap Research* **8** 3–24.

Channel 4 (2008) *Teen Sex Survey*. Available at: http://sexperienceuk.channel4.com/teen-sex-survey (accessed June 2012).

Department of Health (2008) *Health Action Planning and Health Facilitation for People with a Learning Disability: Good practice guidance*. London: Department of Health.

Dickens S, Mitchell M & O'Connor W (2009) *Same-Sex Couples and the Impact of Legislative Changes*. Available at: www.natcen.ac.uk/our-research/research/same-sex-couples/ (accessed June 2012).

Jackson S & Scott S (1996) *Feminism and Sexuality: A reader*. London: CUP. Lifecentre (2012) Gathering Forensic Evidence [online]. Available at: http://www.lifecentre.uk.com/police_info/gathering_forensic_evidence.html (accessed June 2012).

McCarthy M (2009) Contraception and women with intellectual disabilities. *Journal of Applied Research in Intellectual Disabilities* **22** (4) 363–369.

McCarthy M & Thompson D (1997) A prevalence study of sexual abuse of adults with intellectual disabilities referred for sex education. *Journal of Applied Research in Intellectual Disabilities* **10** (2) 105–124.

WHO (2014) *Sexual Health* [online]. Available at: http://www.who.int/topics/sexual_health/en/ (accessed July 2014).

Notes

Notes

Notes

Certificate of achievement

This is to certify that:

....

has achieved ...... hours of study and work-based practice on sexuality and sexual health for individuals with a learning disability by covering the following learning outcomes:

- *Understand the development of human sexuality*
- *Understand how the sexual development of individuals with a learning disability can differ*
- *Understand the issues of sexual health and how these can be supported*
- *Understand relevant legislation influencing the support of sexuality and sexual health for individuals with learning disabilities*
- *Know how to support the sexual expression of an individual with a learning disability*

Signed: ....

Title: ....

Useful contacts

Ann Craft Trust

www.anncrafttrust.org

This organisation is named after the pioneer of sex education work with people with learning disabilities in the UK. It provides advice, information and training on all aspects of abuse and people with learning disabilities.

Brook

www.brook.org.uk

Brook is a national sexual health charity. It provides sexual health services, support and advice to young people under the age of 25 through local centres. This includes people with a learning disability. Their national website provides details of local centres. It also contains information and resources that may help you support individuals.

FPA

www.fpa.org.uk

50 Featherstone Street, London EC1Y 8QU

0207 6085240

This national sexual health organisation has expertise working with people with learning disabilities. It offers staff training courses and has a range of resources targeted at people with learning disabilities.

Image in Action

www.imageinaction.org

Chinnor Road, Bledlow Ridge, High Wycombe HP14 4AJ

01494 481632

Image in Action has been working with people with learning disabilities on sexual issues for over 25 years. It provides direct work with individuals as well as staff training. It has also published a range of useful sex education resources.

The Lucy Faithful Foundation

www.lucyfaithfull.org

Bordesley Hall, The Holloway, Alvechurch, Birmingham B48 7QA

The Lucy Faithfull organisation works to prevent child sexual abuse. It works with perpetrators of sexual abuse and has experience working with men with learning disabilities.

London Lesbian and Gay Switchboard

www.llgs.org.uk

This is a national helpline for people who are lesbian, gay, bisexual or transgendered. It has a database of local organisations, which may be able to provide support to people with learning disabilities, called the Turing Network www.turingnetwork.org.uk.

National Clinical Assessment and Treatment Service

www.nspcc.org.uk

020 7428 1500

This NSPCC resource provides a national service for children and young people up to the age of 21 where concerns exist about sexually harmful or sexually abusive behaviour.